MARINE !FORCE RECON

ASHLEY GISH

SPECIAL FORCES
X
BOOKS

T0004821

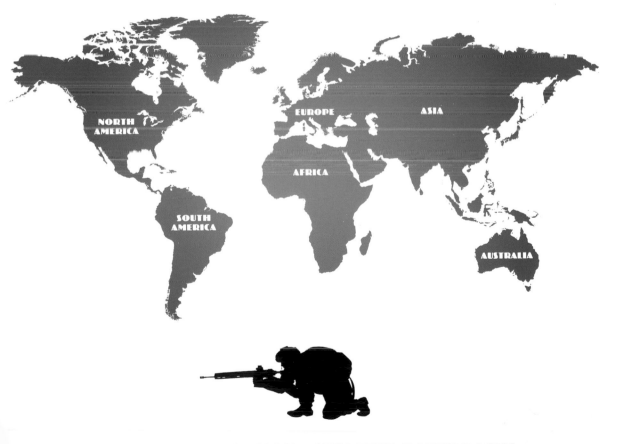

CREATIVE EDUCATION · CREATIVE PAPERBACKS

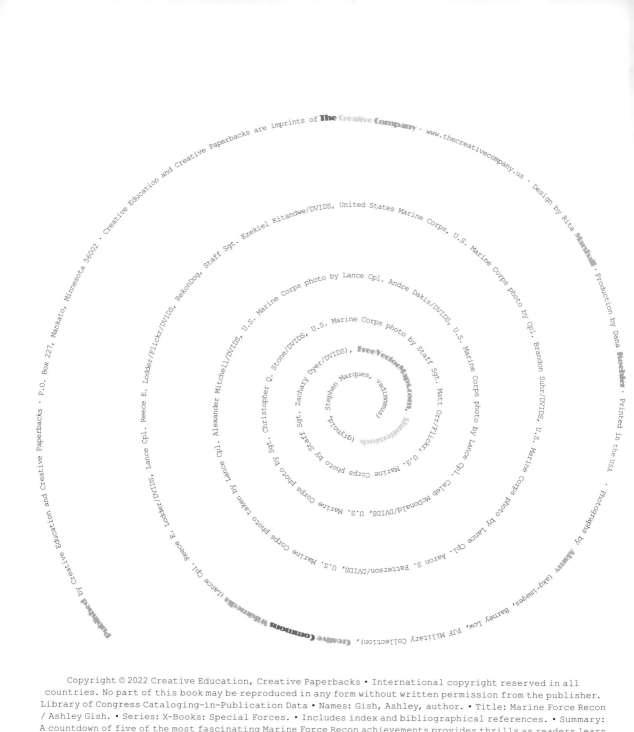

Published by Creative Education and Creative Paperbacks · P.O. Box 227, Mankato, Minnesota 56002 · Creative Education and Creative Paperbacks are imprints of The Creative Company · www.thecreativecompany.us · Design by Rita Marshall · Production by Dana Meachen · Printed in the USA · Photographs by Alamy (aka-images, Barney Low, PJF Military Collection), Creative Commons Wikimedia (Lance Cpl. Reece E. Lodder/DVIDS, Lance Cpl. Reece E. Lodder/Flickr/DVIDS, RekonDog, Staff Sgt. Ezekiel Kitandwe/DVIDS, United States Marine Corps, U.S. Marine Corps photo by Cpl. Brandon Suhr/DVIDS, U.S. Marine Corps photo by Cpl. Caleb McDonald/DVIDS, U.S. Marine Corps photo by Lance Cpl. Aaron S. Patterson/DVIDS, U.S. Marine Corps photo taken by Lance Cpl. Alexander Mitchell/DVIDS, U.S. Marine Corps photo by Lance Cpl. Andre Dakis/DVIDS, U.S. Marine Corps photo by Staff Sgt. Matt Orr/Flickr, U.S. Marine Corps photo by Sgt. Christopher Q. Stone/DVIDS, U.S. Marine Corps photo by Staff Sgt. Zachary Dyer/DVIDS), FreeVectorMaps.com, Shutterstock (grynold), Stephen Marques, vadimmmus)

MARINE !FORCE RECON

CONTENTS

SPECIAL FORCES BOOKS

FROM THE RECON CREED:

The title of Recon Marine is my honor.

Conquering all obstacles, both large and small,

I shall never quit.

To quit, to surrender, to give up is to fail.

To be a Recon Marine is to surpass failure;

To overcome, to adapt and to do whatever it takes

to complete the mission.

XTRAORDINARY FORCE

The United States Marine Corps Force **Reconnaissance** is a unique unit. Known as Force Recon, its operators work in the air, on the ground, and in the water.

Force Recon Basics

Force Recon is a valuable special operations force. It supports other Marine Corps forces by gathering information about enemies. Each Force Recon battalion is attached to a Marine Expeditionary Force (MEF). The unit's primary duties are green operations and black operations.

Recon Marines usually slip in and out of enemy territory without being noticed. Secrecy is especially important for green operations. But Recon Marines are fully capable of using deadly force when necessary.

WORLDWIDE MISSIONS

Force Recon's 1st, 2nd, and 3rd Battalions are based in different locations: Camp Pendleton, California; Camp Lejeune, North Carolina; and Okinawa, Japan. Reserve battalion groups are spread out across the United States.

UNITED STATES
OF AMERICA

CAMP PENDLETON
CALIFORNIA

1st Recon Battalion

JAPAN

OKINAWA

3rd Recon Battalion

CAMP LEJEUNE

NORTH CAROLINA

2nd Recon Battalion

Force Recon participates in Visit, Board, Search, and Seizure (VBSS). These missions require operators to board enemy or pirate ships. VBSS missions can be extremely risky. Pirates are often armed and dangerous.

SECRET MISSIONS

Force Recon is not as well known as other special forces.

Green ops happen near water and in enemy territory. Amphibious missions involve landing along coastlines and beaches. Recon Marines use boats or swim to land. Deep recon requires operators to enter enemy territory. They may travel by foot, parachute into an area, or be dropped off by a helicopter.

Black ops involve direct action. On these missions, Recon Marines are said to "bring the fight to the enemy."

Recon Marines can hide in place for days.

BLENDING IN

FORCE RECON BASICS FACT

Force Recon operators are trained to withstand torture.

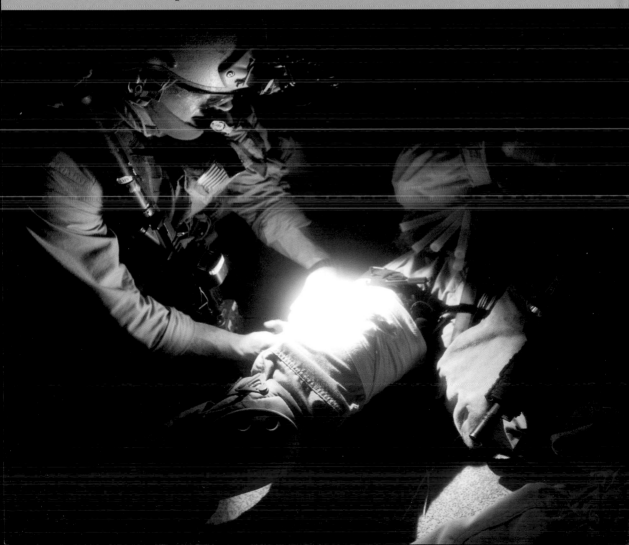

Xtreme Force Recon Achievement #5

Leatherneck Lingo Sometimes, Marines seem to speak their own language. Someone who just finished boot camp is a "Boot." If a Boot talks too much, his commanding officer might tell him to "lock it up," or be quiet. A bad haircut is a "barracks cut." Something you don't understand is "clear as mud." When you do understand, you're "tracking." Cleaning day is also known as "field day."

The nickname "leatherneck" came from the wide, stiff leather collar that was part of the Marine Corps uniform from 1798 to 1872.

Force Recon Beginnings

The first amphibious recon units were assembled during World War II (1939–45). They were called the Marine Raider Battalion and the Observer Group. The units gathered information about enemy beaches.

In 1943, the Observer Group was renamed the Amphibious Reconnaissance Company (ARC). By 1944, ARC had grown and was renamed again. The Amphibious Reconnaissance Battalion boasted 20 officers, 270 **enlisted** men, and 13 medical personnel. It took part in more than 100 missions before the war ended. Though reduced in size, the force continued to carry out missions in other wars. The Amphibious Reconnaissance Battalion's many successes led to the creation of Force Recon.

Force Recon officially became active on June 19, 1957. Recon Marines trained for helicopter and parachute **insertions**. They used these tactics on missions during the Vietnam War (1955–75). After the war, Force Recon was deactivated. It was reactivated in 1986. Four years later, operators were sent to the Middle East for the first Gulf War (1990–91). Since then, the unit has participated in many other missions.

December
1941

June
1966

Observer Group and Raider Battalion assembled

1st Recon Battalion pinned down at the Battle of Hill 488

1990 to 1991

2000 to 2010

Recon Marines assist
in the Persian Gulf War

1st Recon Battalion regroups for
missions in the Middle East

The majority of Force Recon's Vietnam War

missions required helicopter insertions.

Xtreme Force Recon
Achievement #4

First to Command Colonel Bruce F. Meyers
served during the Korean War (1950–53).
In 1957, he became the first commanding
officer of Force Recon. He led 6,300 men
during the Vietnam War. Meyers spent much
of his career developing tactics for
secret Force Recon operations. He was
also a founding member of the Force Recon
Association. The organization supports
Marines and their families. Meyers died
in 2017 at age 91.

XTENSIVE TRAINING

Marines hoping to join Force Recon have a lot to prove. They have to be both fit and smart to make it through training. They must stay calm in unpredictable situations.

LIFE AS A TRAINEE FACT

Recon Marine candidates must have at least

18 months remaining in their term of service.

Basic Reconnaissance Course (BRC)

37.5%

62.5%

drop out or fail

complete BRC

Life as a Trainee

To qualify for training, candidates must pass a challenging physical fitness test. They also need to score 105 or higher on the General Technical section of the timed, multiple choice Armed Services Vocational Aptitude Battery (ASVAB) test. This part of the test covers word knowledge, paragraph comprehension, and mathematical reasoning.

After meeting all the requirements, candidates go on to two-day recon testing. This includes a 550-yard (503 m) swim and a 27-yard (24.7 m) underwater swim. Each candidate performs a deep-water rifle recovery. Then the candidate swims 55 yards (50.3 m) while holding the weapon overhead. Other aquatic tests take place in full gear. Candidates also complete an obstacle course. Many Marines fail this screening the first time, but they can repeat it until they pass.

The Marine Corps was the first branch of the

U.S. military to do helicopter insertions.

XPLOSIVE SKILLS

Those who pass recon screening move on to the 59-day Basic Reconnaissance Course (BRC). During BRC, Marines learn all the skills they will need to carry out recon missions.

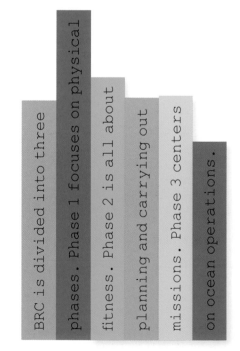

BRC is divided into three phases. Phase 1 focuses on physical fitness. Phase 2 is all about planning and carrying out missions. Phase 3 centers on ocean operations.

In BRC, Marines learn how to travel on the open ocean and land rubber Zodiac boats. They jump out of airplanes and helicopters. They learn to use parachutes, skis, and scuba gear.

Recon Marines are skilled in helicopter rope suspension techniques. These are used for insertions and extractions when a helicopter cannot land. One of the most common is fast-roping. This is when an operator holds the rope with his hands and feet and slides down as fast as possible. A Marine can also coil a rope around his body and slide down it. This is rappelling.

Xtreme Force Recon Achievement #2

Battling Pirates On September 8, 2010, the *Magellan Star* was sailing in the Gulf of Aden off the coast of Yemen when it sent a distress signal. Pirates had taken control of the ship. Early the next morning, 24 Force Recon Marines arrived. Performing VBSS, they boarded the vessel. They stormed the control room. The Marines took the nine hijackers into custody without firing a single shot.

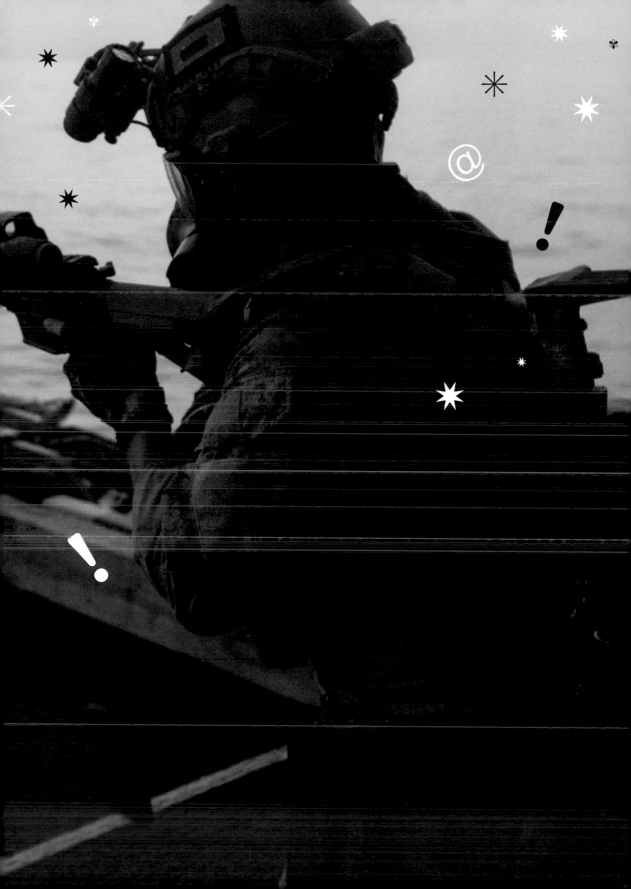

Marines who want to join Force Recon must first pass the Marine rifleman course.

Force Recon Marines are first and foremost Marines. They respect Marines who are not part of the unit.

Recon Marines might use snowshoes or climbing gear on missions in snowy mountains.

On Sting Ray missions during the Vietnam War, Force Recon aggressively attacked the enemy.

While training, it is more important for a candidate to give his best effort than to come in first place.

Thick gloves protect Recon Marines' hands when they fast-rope or rappel.

Additional advanced training courses include sniper and airborne school.

The average age of most new Marine recruits is just 18 or 19 years old.

Helocasting requires jumping into water from a helicopter and swimming to shore.

Force Recon Marines undergo survival, evasion, resistance, and escape training.

All branches of the military use the ASVAB to measure soldiers' strengths and weaknesses.

During recon screening, candidates begin training at 4:30 A.M.

During the Vietnam War, Key Hole missions required silence and secrecy.

In the Vietnam War, Force Recon Marines had a kill rate of

34 enemy soldiers for each of their own.

Xtreme Force Recon
Achievement #1

The Best of the Best Major Jim Capers Jr.
was the first African American to command a
Force Recon team. During the Vietnam War,
he also became the first black man to receive
a field promotion. On one mission, despite
two broken legs, he held off the enemy while
evacuating his men. Capers participated
in 50 black op missions. He was wounded
19 times in 22 years of service. For his
actions in Vietnam, he was awarded the
Silver Star.

GLOSSARY

enlisted – describing people voluntarily enrolled in the military at a rank below officer

insertions – placing troops into an area; getting troops out is called an extraction

reconnaissance – a search to gain information, usually conducted in secret

rucksacks – military backpacks made from strong, waterproof material

RESOURCES

Abdo, Kenny. *United States Marine Corps*. Minneapolis: Abdo Zoom, 2019.

Noll, Elizabeth. *Special Ops Forces*. Mankato, Minn.: Black Rabbit Books, 2017.

"Profile: Marine Special Operations School." Military.com. https://www.military.com/special-operations/profile -marine-special-operations-school.html.

INDEX

Green op missions are considered successful if no shots are fired.